Twitching Hour

Playwright by

Baruch Menache

New York, NY

United States of America

Published by McWest & Associates

ISBN: 978-1-971928-42-5

On Language

Dialogue follows the rhythm of thought more than the structure of conversation.

Words drift, accumulate, and collide.

They should be spoken as though they are only partly under the speaker's control.

Silence is permitted to interrupt.

Dramatis Personae

Jones – A pianist whose words wander in and out of clarity.

Delilah – Striking in presence; hears more than is spoken.

Noah – A man wrestling with the distance between intention and truth.

Samantha – Quick of thought, slow to forget.

Jamie – Sees life sideways; says less than he knows.

George – Friend, skeptic, keeper of unclaimed judgments.

The Gatekeeper – Neither kind nor cruel, simply unmoved.

Grandfather – A voice of past conviction.

Others – Those who pass through the night without settling.

TWITCHING HOUR

An Evening in Several Acts

Act: Bar

*[1960, bar in the city,
Jones speaking to his
manager who is upset]*

Jones

A scented evermore is
language exalting expression;

Them boys will tell ya 'bout it
after a drink that never stops.

[Looking away]

Fainted scent all over the
place,

Sparkling to remember its
name,

Played into hands of a
citation.

[Girl was listening, who was enjoying the performance]

Delilah

> Beckoned, cast for a
> disavowal friendship,
>
> Cloaked imperious to a stand-
> up guy;
>
> Girlish residue of motherly
> breast,
>
> Sanctimonious divergence to
> a fatherless plateau.
>
> Rested the impinged family
> that makes 'self known.

Manager

> Fixed a stable choice
>
> Told a friend in confidence,
>
> Choice no more; friend no
> more.

[Manager leaves]

Delilah

Sand dunes and clothed faces

Wearing scent of the East.

Rested for a millennium,

Wind 'n dirt possessed by
fragile destitute,

To no avail of rain and
budding flowers.

*[Man participates, has
interest in the girl and
uses the chance]*

Jamie

Satisfying urges compensate
memory,

Has the fish filleted on a
traditional diet?

Fatherly comfort on a
beckoned shore?

Sifting oblivion to find the
abyss;

Such memories find
forgetfulness in time

And irrevocable desertion to
present and good.

[Friend of the man who
has some envy]

George

Cover that naked part

Shown too soon,

Rather hidden for a reminder.

Memory 's a funny thing, ain't
it?

Act: The Couple

[Raining, outside the bar, the couple walking]

Noah

Singing in the rain that was meant to pour,

Isn't gratefulness that overcomes tribulation?

Winds washed before having met its shore.

Samantha

Lying awake and knowing

Wherein it wasn't humility

Nor the kind word of a stranger.

But surely given up on
covering

For a lie that stood more than
allotted.

Noah

So you went down to the
bowels of goodness—

Or you thought so to be

Until you noticed a mischief
of mines catching a turn

But you couldn't turn back;

Could you now, could you
now, could you now.

[Changing tone]

You must go forward

Knowing the path is forged
wrong

But that it is your own

And it is comfortable,
righteous and deliberate.

Act: The Gate

[Gatekeeper did not let them in]

Noah

The howling of the maestro at the assembly gate.

'Give back the greens,' a voice of another said.

Shall you take yellows when the world is painted orange?

None shall cover the red that glows in black,

Instead, let us in, naked as we are.

Gatekeeper

The outside is just as good.

Samantha

> Outside is nothing other than
> where we don't belong;
>
> Belong in the fence, destiny in
> the fence, home in the fence.

Noah

> Gates brand me foreigner,
>
> Open what is made to be
> opened,
>
> Allow entrance to believe an
> exit
>
> That we exchange locations,
>
> For outside you look and
> inside I do.

Gatekeeper

> Midst the night you try that
> luck,
>
> Hasn't run out 'suppose you
> now,
>
> Passion'd make way, whatever
> the cause.

If hell is 'round the fence-gate,
shan't you give up?

Come in now, your kind is the
late-comer,

Evening to its next of kin and
children begotten.

Come right in!

[They enter]

Act: Couple at the Bar

[Man struggles with door]

Samantha

Troubled with the door
Ajared to an opening.
Favoring the simple folk
That slip through cracks
Behind fading glimmers
And second-hand hope.

Noah

Rather face the entranceway
Than be damned from earth,
All for an unearthly glance

And a run-outta-luck type of
guy.

> [Sitting, entering an even
> more melancholic state,
> sparse people, its late]

Noah

Trust the Saints and Rabbis

Buckled to worldly pressure,

'Get him to speak our
language',

Ocean depths of weightful
bounty

Telling pupils of sorrow in
light

Shining at the least favorable;

The opposite tale is the better
one.

Samantha

Deluded the senseless, smiled
one's lot

Comprehending the wise
table, smirked the lot.

Noah

Shiny does glimmer in light
Does wine try its match,
Loses in ascendancy,
Claims the jokester's thrill
And suit-man bolster.
Let us ascend then!

Act: The Dance

[Pianist collects himself, as a prelude to his next song]

Jones

Feeble, Yaw! Folken disturbed by spirit,

Spirit! Get the paper trail to admit the tree;

Water the rebellion within the sandlot.

This gets better, as with time in the bygone.

Instinctual mess made of starvation for love,

Bundled warmth forebodes a
ruled child,

Heating the victim's camp
with attention.

[He plays the song]

Will you come

After my hair goes long

Will ya' delight my seat

After a night goes terror

Will you try me twice

Forgive now in pastime.

Rummaging town hall,

Fading blacks, scary greens

Flipped the story just this one time

Swift as promised my dear mind,

*Swinging the dirty glass 'gainst the
wall*

Hesitant for a full panic show.

Will you, will you—

Will you come back to me?

[After the song]

[To the couple, who was being frolic]

Jones

Frequent Tillery grindstones

An iron mold remedies the crush.

Was love conditioned by circumstance?

They tell you: man between worlds.

Others, of the dare-ruling-man

Betwixt a child and fatherly descent.

Samantha

Tell them to be fixtures

For magic has been pronounced.

The names of immortal men

Who fell to see her skin,

Ashamed of the elderly look
That had been so promised.

Jones

Go on soldier of eighteen,

Adjoining youth, missing in
the know,

Makes for the bold.

Trying a passion'd heart,

While giving up on
immortality;

Elders and a pact with
mortality,

Remiss to the four-step
rhythm.

Wiseness comes with a daring
price,

Youth-less to be one of many;

Tales forgotten in the drum-
drum.

[Hits the piano key]

Noah

Chanced a candle in the wind storm,

Sighted lightning from windowpanes,

Sheltered of camp fire to its warmth.

Felt relief of a generation

Awaiting a learning season.

Younglings adore the mature mold,

Safe haven seem grandeur of beards.

Fastidious merits a chosen obsession;

Love knows no bounds,

Save what defiles her grace.

Delilah

Since the day was born

And nighttime etched
memory,

Loss was a forward way

Lest to forget a birthing past.

Jamie

Cloverfield has teething eyes,

Bulging ears, an immortal
smirk.

Principal disfavors the
repulsion of kind.

*[Jones fiddled with the
keys, hummed a tune]*

Jones

To the slippery grace,

Wishing for more — for more

Noah

Shipped on an ocean liner

Defying the bird in sky.

Takes risks by water

Free from human hand

Where rebels find merit;

Stranger to the captain,

Water equal in part.

Wave equal to the squall—

Salt in portion, despair never-
lasting;

The melancholic brain
unstudied.

Jamie

Dropped a penny down the
chute,

Waiting for the drop in the
meanwhile,

Laundry festering in
overshadowing bins.

Spoken a friendly face
disturbed incoming disgrace.

Satiation has its sanitation of
purged senses

Leading right away from the
delirious.

Jones

In the dump, faced down,
chilled to a soda glaze.

Haven't seen ya lately, all
faced in that garbage heap!

You look different, a face
from the scraps.

Don't tell my American doll I
betrayed her gloss.

Frequent a time of clicks
edging ever faster,

Known soldier of reserves;

Whirlwinds' champion a
savior's heart,

Looked upon Rose to give an
extra kiss;

Turnaround, bare-chested and
naked.

They came back. Didn't they?
Simply grand of premonitions.

Prophesize the end just never
the middle

Philosophize the beginning
just never the end

Love the middle rather never
the beginning.

Delilah

Felicity of mind's escapade,

They tell a-right—right from
the inside;

You were rather looking from
the outside.

Finally they came out, ought
with some repose;

Never having met where right
meant something.

Instead, the eagle and its
wingspan carry,

Irrespective, weightless of
your production.

Jones

What's wrong with the
shadow?

Is it so deafening to be
contrast of light?

To offer comparison-view of
the ensemble?

Better than a perked audience

Than the actor who is but a
remedy.

Only with its shadow

Do we taste life,

Never has one gone below

To return with its story.

Awful to the network behind
a connection?

To the web behind a spider?

To darkness that brings forth
day?

To a Duke impressing the
king?

To a Princess humanizing
father?

Noah

The mirrored contrast, what
else can reflect light?

Last place begins the second
race; first, to home.

The top never arrives, save
for the strider.

To touch falls at arms length,
kiss at a breath.

Long game stretched into
submission; game or not.

Short dost leave without
players and dice,

Industry offers perfection of a
sure direction,

The wise barred a union,
prefabricated with no amends.

Samantha

Give me the suit-man,

Give me man or his smile

Don't give me man suited
with a smile.

Delilah

Like a daughter overdrawing
the well

Planting gardens in the
footpath to father,

Or a dock, four seasons
toiled,

Raising flag to her maiden
voyage;

Captains coattails in the
horizon.

Jones

Underserved to be pained by me,

Underscored thy expensive love.

Delilah mustn't deliver the news

Foreboding a large settlement,

Territories renewed of that family bond.

Saturday, the renowned capacity,

Mindful endeavors that do not lay;

The backs of never-endings;

Statured frailness of an exchange.

Isn't that right, Delilah?

Delilah

To be sure.

Jones

Your minute wasn't spent

In the sacrifice of youth.

Hadn't resilience to spiral with
us,

To make way to the bond of
family

And the scarcity of dignity?

[Samantha chuckles]

Just a minute! I will be right
with you!

After that mainstay of
semblance,

To a land forefathers do not
know,

Whence retracted, revised and
revisited,

Though shambled minds of
youth-loads,

Daring State members into
the mines.

I will get to the task, for
tasking is me.

Haven't you the moment to
offer grace?

Of the frailty of you and me,

With a backdrop of that
bond?

Spinning the world you
perform'd,

On this platform of regularity
and punctuality,

To give allowance for another
guy—

The entrance-way a'ready
fulfilled.

A bond, you say, Delilah!

I say yoke of youth;

A promised state of
reminders.

Haven't the warlord lost
nostalgia

In the objective of lost
margins?

To the trekker of seas, to
foreboding novelty?

Haven't the will to remember,
lest to forget.

Never a promise of more, or
less—

In the balance surely not.

He goes by the sword, by the
fight, the endeavor,

To drink the rest of time.

Delilah, you mustn't know
revision,

We may find a path to youth;

Do not act upon it, do not
despair

As sole warrior without a
quest.

Stay—

As we exchange remnants of
dignity.

A moment will come,

Your quest will be made

Neither from stone or welted
concrete,

Nor wood and ironclads.

The composition of love

For your past and my future.

It will shine the heavens

In return for a favor.

Alas, you will get your quest,

Not as solitary warrior,

Headstrong that makes wars

Where likened find shame.

Disgraced for infantile
makeup,

Where no mind need
conjuring

Nor heart for enduring.

For now, my dear Delilah,

Revise and retract but do not
retreat.

Act: Samantha's Charge

Jones

[Turning to Samantha]

Samantha of Sam's charge

Saul's heeded dread

Known not another deed.

Do a mind satiated

Who has an owner

Housing to a child's eye

Crafted to a glow where—

Chambers give brevity.

Down by the dock

Flags brittle in autumn rain,
Sorrow crept the sheet frame
Worldly affairs gone astray.
With three choices, two too
many
On this frightful night
Disguised in white of
oblivion.

Samantha

Try me for a friend
As I make you out to be
More than your liking.

Come be my lover,
To teach me how to love—
Serving the world its next
desert.
Awfully rebounded in
remembrance,

Trailblazing a moonlight
shine.

Near-shoes that do no
walking

Alongside minds mirroring
the horizon.

Trouble my winter

With a recipe of comfort,

Welling in the darkness;

It's the thought that counts.

Selling grace by the pound

Charmed the unease phasing,

Tested to the overture,

Skipped the curtain reveal

Unending the spiraled demise.

Jones

Gone awry,

Piped through clemency,

Disrupted by fate,
Charged through gates
In lovers' chase.

How senseless
Was your word,
Armed with happiness
And joy's jitterbug;
Volcanic ash, simmering.

Samantha

The sensation won't give way
Arching a plethora of rock.
Terrain unraveled,
Crossing the warn'd path,
Inching—pressing feet,
Delirious, provoked and
disrupted.

The tussle of flower buds,

Making for rain that will only
hurt

And dew that will evaporate.

Tranquility not known today,

Stubborn as the next;

Nature's downtrodden.

Weak in spirit gave way to
direction,

An interval of change, better
or worse—

For the better.

Retrace is not for this race,

Calculation for a bygone past,

Enumerating the
embellishment;

A sponging memory-base of
daily renewal.

Seasons tether daytime abode,

Nature at a gridlock in time.

Found in err, lost in prayer;

Heeding to the misery.

Storing a sound memory

If happiness was not an
expense

It'll be there all the same.

Color is flesh, change is
sacrifice.

*[Jones reluctantly
chuckles, strums the keys
in self consciousness]*

Act: Better Times

[Two years prior]

[Their wedding day of the couple, two years prior, sitting at the table together]

Noah's Best Man

Welcome rivals of late!

In late bearings that never hold,

The wedded glare of veil unfolds.

The truest path has scarcely dined,

The ridden road had footage tracked.

Thy nest makers of birded
fowl

Whom sit on treetops teeing
sunrise,

Scarcely referencing nighttime
quietude;

Morning in the palace is
beggars to twilight.

Grandfather

Six sensed a tradition,

Don't believe the shallow
footing,

Gate unlocked to eat
retribution.

Arise from the redemptive
pathway,

Staled its course with a tattoo
too many;

A conversation too long, a
memory too forgotten;

Halted a generation and the
long life wrinkle.

When pages turn unsynchronized

Metered by a two-point stop.

Cornering a bewildered child

Unseemly to innocent eyes.

Two friends—promises upon pavement

Of serving trials to time

As the river dims their thoughts.

[He speaks louder, other listen from other tables, including the bridesmaids]

The depth of consolation,

A truth never to bear,

Young innocence is ever-threatened

To tear something or another

From something or another's arm.

Beheld a moment of void,

The craving of the young

Lest to be born and unwind,

To find fear in the return.

Sadness is a way of progress.

The elders warned

Not to depart the cave,

Or plow the earth and drink
its mead.

They told us the inescapable,

Shan't be the four-legged
forms,

To eat with fork 'n knife.

They told us of depression,

The haunting of the mind.

*[Upset at the dramatic
tone, maid of honor
chimes in]*

Maid of Honor

Mixed berry cocktail,

Tailored garment inches too
long,

Comfort deprived of a single
step;

Wanting to circle a square,

Wanting to profess without
losing privacy;

These are the things that
make wonder without.

[Bride chimes in, giggles]

Bride

Fresh lilacs offer color coded
perfection.

[Enters a drunken cousin]

Noah

Stuttered to a table grace,

Passed knife to a forkful,

Smiled in passing, bewildered
of talk,

Chair scratches wood panels,

Moaning host of delivery
sleep.

Drunken Cousin

See you more in this light,

Mirror startled reflection,

Pay-per-view on dry banks,

Mist to an arid day, rain upon
cold flesh.

Noah

Tested iron, etched into an I-
beam,

Crisscrossing for structural
intact;

Bolted and jolted.

Drunken Cousin

Satirizing the plaintiff stance,

A crisp chuckle molded the
frame

Changeling gives spice to
perspective.

Venoms cruel downpour is
rain two inches over.

'The mess', says the
delinquent in the hall,

Caught the early phase of the
meeting.

Grandfather

[Forced a speech]

The family of the future,

A memory of one's past.

Wholeness for differentiation,

Differentiation for wholeness.

Settlement for exposure

And exposure for settlement.

To do upon a lifetime,

Give grandeur that
reciprocates,

Good-will after it represents,

Kindness where it doesn't.

A travel of regard,

The domicile of substance.

A crowd in dispersal,

Solitude for easy affection.

*[The rest chuckle in
admiration, the cousin
sits down and relaxes]*

Act: Dawn

*[Back at the bar, first
light, houselights dim]*

Noah

When daffodils make rain

Clouds hushed by a little girl's
finger

Commanding legions of iron
men

At waves of devotional heaps.

Jones

Pretty her up spiced for a new
shadow;

Milky-way to find a good
harvest.

Mother to stay mother,

Father mobile with sunlight;

Both pleasured to uncertainty

Of wombs and coattails,

Of style and grace.

George

If he'd tear, mother gave no notice

The way car's oil for vacation day.

Gloss and heels do no second glance

Closeness beholds atomic secrets,

Secreted from memory and a basier shine.

Jones

Shamshackled weirded the feather hat

Scribes keep pen to paper and hand.

The feather, wilted from tears and joy,

'Tis scribe who knows the
winter season

When hats feel burdened of
head gear.

                    [Noah gets up to leave,
                    dreary eyes]

Noah

Alas' away that agony

Of sin and the other one,

Dare say its name.

Given silence to delusions,

Fenced by racketeering.

Chief smiling at the chance,

Told twice, a third for thou;

Shouldered a patterned
charisma.

Sun dripped melancholy

Dared to shelter the horizon.

Color me famous

For my rein is free.

Chocolate dowry

And faithless chance.

[Looking upon his wife]

The brush of shoulder gave
little grace

Or when he desperately gave
chance

At midnight's feast to
demons' presence

Or the moment she gave
repose

To sweetness etched in her
breast.

Most dearest was she, even if
a memory.

Jones

Go now, pave an honest path

Sister years don in plenty.

*[Noah and Samantha
leave]*

[Turning to Delilah]

Lady goodness sit beside me.

Set aside greatness and
mediocrity,

Wanting you primed and
prepped

For good spice and evil rice.

I come from heaven and hell,

Don't know the other,

Or the bridge between them.

I was raised to be wasteful of
bridges,

Arching their way to other
arches.

[Delilah, George and
friend leaves]

[To himself]

Intermingled to pray for
strength

Amidst a morning cry

And soft wind against their
face.

Wanderin' selfless fortunes,

To make de' mark of man,

Find favor in aristocratic folk,

In baptism of a Victorian
Church,

That'll post without a battle
cry,

Or verse of stable meaning,

Reining the world without an
empire.

> *[Going outside, looking
> at the people]*

Dearest, off you go in
Monday's light,

Piercing corners, bodegas first
bite,

Sifting in the a.m., delivery in
the p.m.,

Doorways, circular to
singular,

Daring folk and meager folk,

Stationed people and mobile
persons;

Four hours to the gates
unlocked;

Tap to run no more dry.

Author

Baruch Menache writes at the intersection of narrative, philosophy, and lyric expression. His work spans poetry, essays, and theatrical pieces that examine the interior life and its many thresholds. He lives in New York with his wife and children.